Photographing
PLANTS
AND GARDENS

Photographing PLANTS

AND GARDENS

 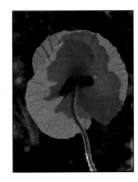 

PHOTOGRAPHS AND TEXT BY

John Doornkamp

DESIGNED BY GRANT BRADFORD

FOUNTAIN PRESS

To Margaret, who, amongst many other good things,
showed me how to value plants and gardens.

Published by
FOUNTAIN PRESS LIMITED
Fountain House
2 Gladstone Road
Kingston-upon-Thames
Surrey KT1 3HD

Text and Photographs
JOHN DOORNKAMP

Designed by
GRANT BRADFORD
Design Consultants
Tunbridge Wells
Kent

Colour Origination
HBM Singapore

Printed and Bound
in Italy by *SFERA*

ISBN 0 86343 363 4

CONTENTS

INTRODUCTION

This book is written for anyone who enjoys making a photographic record of the beauty that they find in gardens and plants. It doesn't matter whether you consider yourself primarily to be a gardener or photographer, this book is aimed at both.

What follows does not demand a technical knowledge about either gardening or photography. It does, however, assume a love of creativity and beauty, and perhaps a willingness to master a few basic skills that will ensure success in this branch of photography.

Over the years I have come to realise that the best place in which to learn the necessary skills for photographing plants is in your own garden. It has the singular advantage of being close to home! No time is lost getting there, advantageous light conditions can be used when they occur, and you know your own plants. As your photographic skills develop they can then be applied to gardens which you visit – where time for experimentation may be limited.

Good garden and plant photography comes from both the ability to see a strong picture and from a sound basic knowledge of photography. Of these two abilities the hardest to acquire is the 'seeing eye'. Fortunately many gardeners have it naturally – that is why they are good gardeners. This book is designed to show how the seeing eye and a competence in photography can be brought together to create memorable pictures.

The photography of gardens and plants is different from many other kinds of photography in that there is a greater control over the subject than is the case, for example, with landscape photography or in the photography of wildlife. You can design your planting so that certain colour or plant texture combinations are brought together. You can position pot plants in such a way that a pleasing arrangement is created. These are controls that you should exercise.

This observation has a serious implication. It means that some of your gardening will be done in order to benefit your photography – you have given yourself two intertwining hobbies. As you carry out your planting you think about the potential for good photographic images. As you carry out your photography you think about what you can do in the garden in order to create an even more pleasing result. In time the two thought processes become inseparable.

Only a comparatively brief description is given here of cameras and other equipment. A fuller account is given in the companion volume in this series by Paul Hicks, Photographing Butterflies and Other Insects.

Any particular uses of equipment will be described at the appropriate place in the text.

For those of you who are interested, the photographs were taken in my own garden unless otherwise stated.

The ultimate aim of garden and plant photography is to generate images that record the beauty of the garden and its plants. In doing so you will have many hours of frustration, all of which will vanish when you achieve those images that delight. Persevere and they will be yours. Follow the guidelines in this book and they will be yours sooner rather than later.

I wish you as much joy as I have had in photographing plants and gardens.

John C Doornkamp, Nottingham

YOUR APPROACH TO GARDEN PHOTOGRAPHY

Your approach to garden photography will be as individual as your taste in gardens and plants. Gardens, like photographs, provoke an emotional response which is neither objective nor rational. Sometimes we may even know that we like a garden without being able to define exactly why this is so. Our taste in gardens is individual and our approach to garden photography will reflect this.

It is useful to consider gardens and plants on several scales, moving progressively from a general view of a garden right down to the photography of a single flower. Every aspect is rich in photographic opportunities.

HINT– *Make a habit of looking at your garden at all scales from the very general to the very detailed.*

When you go into the garden with your camera stand at one end of the garden and view the garden as a whole. Move about until you have the best vantage point, and take a photograph. Now concentrate on finding the best viewpoint for sections of the garden which include whole flower beds, and take another photograph. Now repeat this process for each border, the patio area, the pond, the individual plants and then the flowers. In this way you will see all of the different facets of the garden that merit a photograph. Repeat this process through the seasons.

Alan Bloom's garden at Bressingham in Norfolk, England, is known as the Dell Garden. It is too large to photograph as a whole, but this section is typical of its nature in June. An overcast sky gave even lighting with no harsh shadows. The yellow leaves of the tree in the background provide a focal point. The viewpoint was chosen so that the most colourful elements in the composition occurred near the central line of the image.

Ornamental features in gardens can include pots, gates, statues, gnomes, fountains, bird baths, and many others. These are 'hard' features compared with the 'soft' forms of the plants. They have usually been placed in the garden where the gardener thinks that they look attractive.

The photographic challenge is to create a pictorial image that reflects the gardener's intentions. This is all very subjective, as is most gardening and garden photography. In the case of this photograph, within the Butchart Gardens on Vancouver Island, Canada, there has been a purposeful intent to show off the corner with the pot, the gate and the group of bright red flowers, by throwing out-of-focus the flower bed in the background. This is achieved by using a low f-number (i.e. a wide aperture) on the camera, and focusing on the ornamental gates and pot.

Ponds provide a special photographic opportunity, as well as a challenge. They provide an environment for a range of plants that do not occur elsewhere in the garden, as well as a habitat for fish, frogs, newts and other wildlife. The surface of the water can provide subtle reflections, but it can also throw out a strong reflection of the sun that completely fools the exposure meter, so be careful. Here care has been taken to avoid any such bright reflections from the water, though the low-angle sun does give added 'life' to the lily leaves in the background.

The photographic techniques appropriate to each scale of viewing differ in certain respects. They all demand correct exposure, competence in composition and accuracy in focusing. However, the techniques required for views of a whole garden are very different from those required for close-up plant photography. We need to establish the essential techniques appropriate to each case and this will be done in the chapters that follow.

There are, nevertheless, some useful hints and tips that can be given that are applicable no matter what the scale of the subject. Make these a matter of habit, and your success rate will improve almost at once.

TIP– *Compose the photograph with care.*

Check what is in the viewfinder – especially watch out for those unwanted intrusions that creep in at the edges.

TIP– *Use a tripod.*

There are two causes of blurred photographs: the subject moves or the camera moves. If the camera is firmly mounted on a tripod then it won't be the camera, and all you have to do then is to control the movement of the subject (more of that later!).

TIP– *Take several exposures.*

Sometimes it is very difficult to gauge the correct exposure, so be prepared to take three images in each case – one at the exposure indicated by the exposure meter, one slightly darker and one slightly lighter.

TIP– *Some of the best images are taken on dull, overcast days.*

We tend to assume that the best images result from photographing in bright sunlight. This is not always the case. Much better results may come from photographing in a diffuse, even slightly misty, light.

TIP– *Think carefully about why you are taking a particular photograph.*

The purpose for which a photograph is intended should influence the way in which you carry out the photography and the nature of the film that you use.

Each of these tips will be expanded upon again later in the book.

Single flowers can only stand out really well if they contrast with their backgrounds. In this case the image is simplified and the flower shown off to advantage by rendering the background almost black. This has been achieved by exposing for the bright flower (making sure it had a dark background), and limiting the depth of field of the image by using a low f-number. Since the exposure was set to provide a true rendering of the flower the darkness of the shadow area then fell outside the range of the sensitivity of the film, making it appear as black.

Some photographers enjoy the challenge of making images of plant detail. It is a real challenge! This photograph gets close to the rose, allowing it to fill the frame. By the time we are dealing with this level of detail the rest of the garden becomes irrelevant.

Colour combinations are an important part of photographic composition, as they are in the colour scheme of gardens and flower beds. Here, in the gardens of Wollerton Old Hall, Shropshire the colours have been chosen by the gardener. The photograph attempts to show the combination of blue, green and pink that gave this part of the flower bed its character.

THE IMPORTANT ROLE OF LIGHT

Apart from the plants themselves the single most important thing for good garden photography is advantageous lighting conditions. This does not necessarily mean strong direct sunlight. In some circumstances the best light may occur during a shower or when there is an overcast sky. The 'ideal' light depends on what you are photographing.

In general, it is better to photograph gardens and flower beds in an overall even light. The kind of light that does not throw harsh shadows, creating dark featureless areas which always look bigger and uglier on the photograph than they did in reality. An even light occurs when it is raining.

People are surprised when they see someone taking photographs in the rain, although it is not such a good idea during a heavy downpour. Immediately after the rain has stopped and before the sun comes out again, there is often an even diffuse light which does not throw shadows and allows many plants to be photographed in their true colours.

Of course, there is a time when bright light is preferable. This is often the case when photographing individual plants or plants in pots. Bright sunlight can provide a luminance that brings out the colour of the brighter plants, or the structure of the duller plants.

Special photographic effects can be obtained when the plant or flower is lit from behind. This back light shows up the translucence of petals and leaves. It can enrich the colour of the leaves of a copper beech, or the petals of a clematis. Some very good and powerful photographs can be obtained by using back-lighting from the sun.

TIP– Be careful when photographing towards the sun.

Three problems can arise when photographing towards the sun. First and most important, if you look into the sun through the viewfinder it can damage your eyes. Secondly, if you point the exposure meter directly at the sun it can damage the meter. Thirdly, photographing towards the sun

The use of back-lighting can be particularly effective if used with single flowers whose petals have a translucent nature. The back-light on this poppy also serves to pick out the details of the wrinkles in each of the petals, though this is less noticeable where the petals overlap and produce a double thickness through which the light cannot penetrate so easily.

can cause flare through the camera lens which will leave one or more circular areas of brightness on your photograph.

TIP– *Flare can be avoided.*

Use a lens hood, but if you can stand in a shadow (e.g. of a tree) that is even better. Try to get the effect that you want by pointing the camera at an angle to the sun, and catch the back-light from a more side-on position.

It is impossible to control what the sun is doing in the sky. However, it is possible to help things along a bit by encouraging the light that we want to fall where we want it. For example, a reflector can be used to throw light into areas of shadow or on to the plant itself. Reflectors are available commercially, and come in a range or reflective surfaces and colours (e.g. silver, white, gold).

TIP– *Make a home-made reflector.*

Rather than buying a reflector, you can make your own out of white card with or without a covering of silver foil that has been crumpled and then smoothed out again. In fact, one side can carry the foil in order to provide a bright reflection of light, whilst the other side can be left white so as to provide a more diffuse reflected light.

Bodnant Gardens in North Wales belongs to the National Trust. It comprises over 80 acres of formal gardens, woodlands, water features and especially, as shown here, rhododendrons and azaleas. The problems with trees and large bushes is that they cast shadows when direct sunlight falls on them. In this case the problem has been avoided by photographing in the rain. This kind of diffuse light is especially good when photographing large portions of a garden.

These primulas were taken immediately after the rain had stopped. The diffuse light of the still overcast sky has not only prevented the development of shadows, but has also allowed the colour of these flowers to be rendered true on the film emulsion. There is a tendency in harsh light for colour to deviate, although it may still be perfectly acceptable.

Sometimes the problem is not that the plant needs a boost in light but that it needs a softer light. Such diffuse light is provided by cloud cover. However, when no cloud cover is available it may be necessary to use a diffusing screen. Commercial versions are available, such as a gauze-type of material stretched across a frame. This cuts out the glare of direct sunlight and provides the required diffuse light.

TIP– Make a home-made diffuser.

A diffuser can be made out of a variety of materials including muslin or tracing paper fastened across a frame of about one metre square. In an emergency you can ask someone to hold a stretched out white linen handkerchief between the sun and the plant or flower.

DETERMINING THE CORRECT EXPOSURE

Most photographers rely on the exposure determined by the in-built exposure meter on their camera. Exposure consists of two parts: the size of the opening that permits the light into the camera (the aperture), and the shutter speed which determines the length of time over which light falls on to the film. For a specific light intensity the larger the aperture the shorter the required shutter speed (and vice-versa).

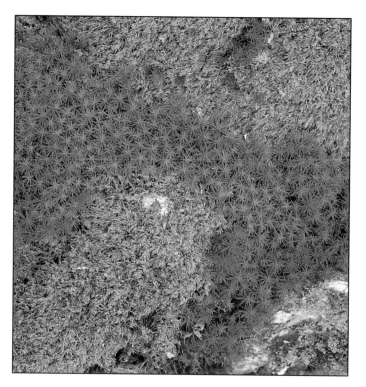

Mosses seem to photograph particularly well after it has rained. The interest in the photograph is not provided by colour but by pattern. Whilst it is tempting to always photograph the bright and cheerful, there are many fine images to be made amongst the pastel shades and subdued colours. For these a diffuse light is nearly always best.

On some cameras, such as a 35mm single-lens reflex (SLR) with manual controls, it is possible for the user to set any combination of aperture and shutter speed. This gives an important additional control over the nature of the image that is produced (this is discussed again later). With many compact cameras the aperture and shutter speed settings are 'hidden' from the user, and this imposes severe limitations on the usefulness of these cameras for serious garden and plant photography.

There are some circumstances when the exposure meter does not provide a good indication of the exposure setting that should be used. For example, a scene that contains snow is likely to finish up too dark in the photograph because the exposure meter thinks the snow is mid-grey in colour and fails to let enough light in to allow the final image to show snow as white. Similarly, a black object, or even a very dark flower, will be interpreted by the exposure meter as having the reflectance of a mid-grey tone, and the result will be an over-exposed image because the camera has allowed too much light on to the film in an attempt to show the object as grey rather than as black.

Side lighting is catching these tulips and strengthening their colour. A camera angle has been adopted so that the only thing that lies behind these flowerheads is shadow. That way there is nothing to detract from the impact produced by the strong directional light.

TIP– *Use a hand-held incident-light meter to determine exposure and set the aperture and shutter speed accordingly.*

The function of an incident-light meter is to measure the intensity of the light falling on a plant rather than the amount of light reflected from that plant. The value given by the incident meter is therefore independent of the colour of the plant itself, and thus will give a truer exposure reading. This approach is only possible, of course, where the camera allows independent settings to be made.

TIP– *With a fully automated camera point the lens towards a mid-tone object (at the same distance from the camera as the plant you are going to photograph) and half depress the shutter button. Then turn the camera to the subject of your photograph and make the final pressure on the button.*

In most cases automatic cameras will 'hold on to' the exposure that it calculates for the area in the centre of the frame when the shutter is half depressed. If this is an object with a mid-tone reflectance then this is the exposure that will be used for the picture that you take. Be careful though, for the camera will also use the same distance setting as that for the selected mid-tone object. Make sure,

These yellow tulips have been treated in the same way as the red tulips in that they have been set against a dark background. This time the light is coming from almost directly behind the flowers and shining through the petals rather than on to them.

therefore, that the mid-tone object and your final object are an equivalent distance from the camera.

THE USE OF SHUTTER SPEED

Where there is a freedom to determine the shutter speed to be used, what are the circumstances that control its value?

Since the greatest enemy of good plant photography is movement caused by the wind, there is an obvious need to use a shutter speed which is fast enough to freeze any movement. Normally this would be a speed of about 1/125 second or faster.

TIP– A useful rule of thumb is to take the focal length of the lens double it and convert it to its inverse and use this value as the shutter speed.

As an example, if the lens has a focal length of 50mm, doubling this would make it 100, and the inverse of this is 1/100 second. If the camera does not have that specific value as a shutter speed go for the next fastest available speed (in this case it might be 1/125 second). This approach also kills camera shake which can arise from the photographer moving the camera whilst the photograph is being taken.

The greater the shutter speed the smaller the aperture has to be in order to provide the correct exposure. This has its own set of consequences.

Photographer Clive Nichols demonstrates how to use a reflector to brighten up the underneath of flowers when the contrast between the top of the flower and the underneath of the petal, which is in shadow, is too great for the film to accommodate.

THE USE OF APERTURE SETTINGS

Aperture is measured in terms of f-numbers. These usually run in sequence 3.5, 5.6, 8, 11, 16, 22, with extensions beyond these limits in some cases. The smaller the available aperture value the faster the lens is said to be. What this means is that the smaller the aperture number the greater the amount of light that is let through on to the film.

Since exposure is a balance between shutter speed and aperture it follows that if the shutter speed is fast the size of the aperture must be greater than when the shutter speed is slower, if the same amount of light is to be let through on to the film in each case.

Unfortunately, photographic life is not as simple as that. Larger apertures bring limitations. For example, the larger the aperture the shorter the depth of field. Thus, if you photograph a flower bed with a large aperture (i.e. with a low f-number), it is more likely that some of the foreground and some of the background will be recorded out of focus than if you had used a smaller aperture (i.e. a higher f-number).

The art of correct exposure settings, therefore, also becomes an art in the selection of depth of field without introducing the movement created by either wind or camera shake.

TIP– Use a tripod to increase your freedom in the choice of shutter speed and aperture combinations.

The strongest component of this image is undoubtedly the way the light falls on the white pampas grasses. However, the view is so much towards the sun that an octagonal flare spot has developed just above and to the right of the grasses. Be warned, flare like this can spoil a good picture, avoid the problem by using a lens hood or by pointing the camera further away from the sun. I clearly failed to do either! If you have not got a lens hood with you try to stand with the camera in the shade of a tree or a large bush.

The use of a tripod will eliminate the problem of camera shake. It will also make it easier to compose the photograph, and to allow you to take several exposures of the same features with a range of shutter speed and aperture combinations.

THE USE OF FLASH

Many cameras are fitted with built-in flash units. It is very tempting to photograph flowers using flash. There is the feeling that to do so will brighten them up and give a stronger image. Not so, the use of flash invariably ruins the colour balance of plant and background and leads to a very harsh image. The usual result is disappointment with the final photograph.

HINT– Use flash with discrimination, and preferably only in close-up situations.

EXPOSURE AND CLOSE-UP PHOTOGRAPHY

As the subject of your photography gets closer and closer to the camera it is more and more likely that the exposure meter will give an over-estimate of the amount of light reaching the film. In other words, the image will be under-exposed.

TIP– Cover yourself by taking close-ups at several exposures, starting with the metered reading and then increasing the exposure gradually for the next four images.

PHOTOGRAPHING GARDENS

A long view of Allan Bloom's Dell Garden at Bressingham in Norfolk, England. A sense of balance is retained in the composition by having tall trees on both sides of the picture. A focal point is provided by the bright spot in the centre distance. The soft morning light (around 07.15hrs in June) is not strong enough to throw shadows, and that helps to maintain an even density of light and shade throughout the picture. The telephoto zoom lens was set at a focal length of 100mm. This has the effect of fore-shortening the distance and narrowing the width of the image. However, this focal length was chosen on purpose so that distracting elements to the side were missed out and both the tree trunk and the copper-coloured leaves were kept in.

The instinctive reaction of the photographer in a beautiful garden is to raise the camera to the eye and to start clicking away. At the time it is great fun, but when the results come back from the processing laboratory there is usually a sense of disappointment. Why should this be so?

The three most common reasons for disappointment are: that the picture is too confused; that the flowers and plants are too small; and/or that the shadows are too strong, producing ugly dark patches.

TIP– Do not include too many elements in one picture.

Confusion occurs because there is too much to look at. Colours and patterns can easily conflict with each other, and their greater compactness on the photograph, as compared to the wider expanse of the garden itself, increases the sense of confusion to the eye.

TIP– Avoid great ranges of light and dark within one picture.

Photographic film is unable to record the same range of light and dark tones that our eyes can take in when we are looking at a garden. As a result the darker areas tend to come out unacceptably dark, or even as black, and the lighter areas are unacceptably light.

A focal point can be provided by strong light on a bright colour, as seen here with a strong afternoon sun falling on bright red tulips.
The sense of balance is kept by the low bush on one side and the group of long leaves in the pond on the opposite side.

Left: Another view of a part of the Dell Garden. It is not possible to photograph it all at once. This time the camera has been turned on to its side (called 'portrait format') so that the sense of the trees rising above the ornamental pond could be included. The early morning sun provides a warm light, which gives a richer glow to the colour of the plants than would occur with a bright midday sun. The yellow flowers in the foreground, the red flowers on the wall, and the light on the tree provide a continuing sense of depth within the picture.

In reality it is generally not possible to photograph a whole garden all at once. The camera simply cannot take it in, unless it is a very small garden photographed from a high viewpoint with a very wide-angle lens.

Although choosing a high viewpoint is not always an option (and few of us would get on to the roof in order to photograph the garden), we do have choices of viewpoint. This choice is a very important component in garden photography.

TIP– *Think very carefully about the choice of viewpoint.*

Despite the instinct to raise the camera on first sight, don't do it. Take time to walk around a garden. Get to know it, and in particular get to know what it looks like from the range of available viewpoints. You will soon discover the location from which the garden is seen to best advantage.

There is nothing special about this suburban garden, yet photographing it calls upon the same set of skills as photographing a large magnificent garden that is a public showpiece. The composition has been chosen so that there is a sense of balance (there is colour interest as well as structural elements on each side) and a focal point (the white seat) at the end of a set of steps. Not a great picture, but pleasing because it is balanced, has a point of interest and is taken in a light that picks out the colour without creating harsh shadows. It is fortunate that the yellow of the tulips is set against a dark background, it helps them to stand out and there is nothing behind them to compete for our attention. You do need some luck in the way that individual components of a garden lie in relation to each other. As the photographer you cannot take it upon yourself to rearrange another person's garden. When it comes to photographing your own that is a completely different matter. You can garden to suit your photography!

The most important components in this will turn out to be not only the compositional elements of the garden but also the nature of the light which is present at the time.

The two most important features of good composition in a garden photograph are a sense of balance and a focal point.

A different approach to composition is used here. The garden is at Burford House in Shropshire just west of Tenbury Wells, England. The early morning winter light falling across the lake gave a special glow. A view straight across the lake was boring, so the tree trunk and the wooden bench were included in the foreground in order to add interest. It was a case of looking round until the best view of the lake was found. No film could provide an acceptable exposure for both the light on the lake and the shadow areas of the wooden bench, so the choice was made to let the bench be recorded in silhouette and to keep the light on the lake as true as possible.

Compositional balance occurs either through a balance of colours or a balance of the main structural forms such as bushes and trees. If colours clash a sense of imbalance occurs. If one large tree or bush dominates one side of the picture, a sense of imbalance may also occur, but for a different reason. Balance has to be judged as you look through the viewfinder.

HINT– *Before pressing the shutter think about the balance in the image.*

A classic approach to the composition of a garden photograph is to point the camera straight down a path between two parallel flower beds, at the end of which there stands a prominent statue. In other words, not only is there a symmetry in the balance (provided by the two parallel flower beds) but there is also a focal point towards which the eye is drawn.

TIP– *Always include a strong focal point in a garden photograph.*

The focal point does not have to be a statue. It can be a distinctive tree, a colourful bush, a bright flower bed, or a waterfall. It always helps to have something quite distinct in the background to carry the eye through the garden to the far point. This is further enhanced if you can find a line of something (it may be a path, a flower bed, a colourful or shapely hedge) that leads the eye towards the focal point. This is all part of obtaining a pleasing composition that has a structure rather than being random clutter.

Something that none of us can escape in the photography of gardens is the effect of different lenses. Things can get very technical at this point, but they need not do so. Let us start with a question. Do you know the focal length of the lens of your camera? It is important that you should. The reasons are that the focal length affects both the width of the image and the sense of depth within the picture. For example, on a 35mm camera a lens with a focal length of 50mm is reckoned to provide a 'normal' view. If the focal length is less than this the breadth of the picture will be greater and the sense of depth within the picture will also increase. If the focal length is greater than 50mm the width of the picture will decrease and the sense of depth becomes compressed. These tendencies increase the further the focal length of the lens departs from 50mm.

What this means in practice is that a long shot down a garden towards a focal point, such as a statue, will look very different if a 28mm focal-length lens is used rather than a 180mm focal-length lens. The wide angle lens (i.e. the 28mm lens) not only takes in more of the view to each side, it also increases the sense of distance and depth in the picture. The telephoto lens of 180mm will narrow the view, increase the size of the object that forms the focal point, and compress the sense of depth within the picture.

If you have a camera that takes interchangeable lenses (or a compact camera with a zoom lens) you have to make a conscious choice as to how you want the final image to look, bearing in mind these lens properties. You need to understand these focal-length characteristics so that you can work with them when doing your garden photography.

PHOTOGRAPHING FLOWER BEDS AND BORDERS

This border in the Dell Garden at Bressingham, Norfolk, England, was dominated by poppies so it seemed appropriate to concentrate on them. The picture has been kept simple by ignoring other elements, and in particular by leaving out every other colour except green, a colour which complements the red very well. The camera angle was chosen so that the early morning light played through the poppies.

The photography of flower beds and borders takes our thinking to smaller portions of the garden, but the principles of composition remain the same. It helps to maintain a sense of balance in the composition, and it may be important also to retain a focal point in the picture.

It really does pay to take care over composition. It is all too easy to become enthusiastic about the colour or forms within a border and to take the photograph without adequate care over composition.

TIP– Choose a viewpoint so that there is good foreground interest.

The plants or features in the foreground can strongly influence the success of your photograph. Try to keep the foreground interesting without introducing elements that are very 'busy'. Fussy foregrounds do not work, simple ones do.

HINT– If there is a plant with a prominent colour be careful to select a background for it that does not clash with it or compete for attention.

Try to give a bright plant a subdued background. Whatever the colour of the plant, try to avoid a colour clash with the

plant behind it (although if this occurs it may say more about the gardener than it does about your photography!).

HINT– *If there is a plant with a prominent structure be careful to select a plain background.*

If the subject of the photograph has a distinct twiggy structure, frame it against a plain background so that the nature of that structure can be clearly seen. It also helps to choose a background with a quiet and complimentary colour so that the shape of the structure is enhanced.

TIP– *Be prepared to get down on one knee, or stand up a ladder, if either improves the viewpoint.*

Too many of us have a fixation about taking every photograph from the height of the human eye. A better composition may be found by getting lower or higher. Try various alternatives in the up-and-down direction as well as in the side-to-side direction.

Depth of field is always an important issue in garden and plant photography. What is meant by this is that on the whole we like everything to be in sharp focus from the front to the back of the picture. Sometimes it is possible to get away with a fuzzy foreground and a sharp background, or vice-versa, but only in very special

This picture is verging on the very confused. It is saved by the contrast between the flowers and the foliage. Bright sunlight was important in this case as it enhanced the vividness of the reds.

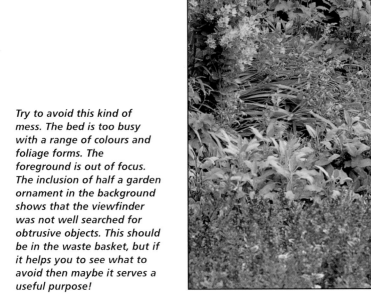

Try to avoid this kind of mess. The bed is too busy with a range of colours and foliage forms. The foreground is out of focus. The inclusion of half a garden ornament in the background shows that the viewfinder was not well searched for obtrusive objects. This should be in the waste basket, but if it helps you to see what to avoid then maybe it serves a useful purpose!

circumstances. It is usually best to aim for maximum sharpness throughout.

TIP– Use the largest aperture at which you can set your camera, this will provide maximum depth of field.

There are special cases where this tip is inappropriate and we shall come to those later. On the whole, however, when photographing beds and borders stick to this tip unless you have good reason for doing otherwise. In general, the higher the f-number (i.e. on the aperture control, see the camera manual) the greater the depth of field (i.e. the greater the range of distances that will appear to have an acceptable sharpness). Those with a compact camera may be unable to alter the aperture setting.

TIP– Focus the lens on a point about one-third of the distance into the picture.

There are rather complex reasons why this is a good idea. It is all to do with focusing on the hyperfocal distance. Since every lens has an acceptable range of focus on either side of the point on which the camera is focused, some of that ability is lost if we always focus on infinity. To retain a

maximum depth of field the hyperfocal distance has to be calculated, but as a rule of thumb a distance one-third of the way into the picture will normally suffice for the photography of gardens, beds and borders.

A frequent reason for disappointment with photographs in the garden is that things have crept in which we did not intend, or of which we were not aware. This is often the case in the photography of beds and borders. Twigs which we did not see lying on the ground stand out as ugly objects on the photograph. Obtrusive branches suddenly appear in the sky when we get our photographs back. They were there, of course, but we did not notice them. The moral is obvious, we should be more careful at the time the photograph is taken.

TIP– *Before every photograph get into the habit of searching round the scene (through the camera viewfinder) and make sure there are no unwanted obtrusive items that will jar the moment you get the results back.*

Searching the viewfinder must become second nature if you want to avoid the intrusion of ugly objects. There is a further consequence to doing this. It is amazing how many

The way to avoid messy pictures of beds is either to find a bed which is itself quite simply planted, and therefore forms a good subject without confusion, or to concentrate on a part of the bed which provides a simple composition. Here the solid mass and strong outline of the moss-covered boulder was used as a foil to the plants. This one part of the bed is enough to show the nature of the rest. It is a better composition than could have been achieved by photographing the bed as a whole.

Here, at Sudeley Castle, England, the gardener has placed yellows reds and light purples together with a large amount of green that I found attractive and therefore wanted to photograph. By filling the foreground with the width of the bed, and allowing the edge of the curved lawn to come into the photograph, the eye is led along the bed.

The same set of plants have been used in another part of the garden at Sudeley Castle, and this time I elected to take the bed face-on, with a hint of the castle building kept in the background.

weeds you will see through the viewfinder, whilst composing a picture, which you did not see when you last did the gardening. The moment that weed is pulled out the two hobbies of gardening and photography have really come together!

HINT– Searching the viewfinder is much easier to do if the camera is mounted on a tripod.

This also has the added advantage that you can go and remove the unwanted twig, cigarette packet, or whatever, without losing your camera position.

PHOTOGRAPHING TUBS, POTS AND PATIOS

Above: This patio shot, which includes one terracotta flower pot, is very simple in composition.
This is the secret of garden photography – keep it simple.

Left: A statue can form the subject of a garden photograph as well as being a focal point in a long view of a garden, bed or border. In this case the choice has been to show the statue in its context, rather than concentrating on the statue in isolation. It is the context which is of interest to the gardener, and in compositional terms it also makes a more pleasing photograph this way.

Some of the most interesting subjects in a garden, in photographic terms, are tubs, pots, ornaments, and troughs which, though they may be used anywhere in a garden, are particularly prominent on patios.

Such features of adornment may contain plants, or they may be free-standing having an ornamental contribution to make in their own right. Whichever is the case, they can make very good subjects in garden photography.

The properties of tubs and pots that matter to the garden photographer include their shape and colour, the plants that they contain, and the fact that they can be moved around. This last attribute is particularly important during the composition of a photograph (say of a portion of a patio), when it may matter how the objects and colours are arranged. It may transpire that the arrangement that makes a good photographic composition is also the arrangement that should have been there in the first place. The result is that a bit more gardening has been done during the course of photography!

TIP– *Do not assume that strong sunlight is the best light for photographing hard objects and ornaments in the garden.*

35

Bright sunlight is almost certainly not the best light for photographing these objects. The main reason is that, unlike plants, they have hard edges and solid bodies that throw strong shadows in the bright sunlight.

HINT– It may be better to photograph a patio immediately after a shower of rain, whilst the sky is still overcast.

Taking photographs of or on a patio can play some tricks on the photographer. If the stone or brickwork is especially light in colour this may reflect the sun. This may not be a bad thing in that the reflected light can soften otherwise harsh shadows. The same can occur with light reflected by the windows of a house.

Garden ornaments can provide very good photographic subjects, they certainly should not be ignored.

A common sight in many gardens in England, the pelargonium in a pot. There was no need to include the whole pot, but it was important not to cut off the top of the plant. The background has been allowed to go out of focus so as to make the flowers stand out, since they are, after all, the main subject of the picture.

PHOTOGRAPHING PLANTS

What could be brighter? A cover of yellow-and-red flowers in bright sunlight. The air was calm and the late afternoon summer light was coming in at a low angle but with considerable intensity.

The gardener thinks of plants in terms of their names, their care, how hardy they are, when the flowers will appear, what their colour and structure will be, how they will fit in to the overall scheme of things and the diseases and infestations to which they are subject. The photographer shares with the gardener only a limited number of these concerns, namely the attributes that relate to colour, shape and texture. These are the elements of plants which, when subjected to the right light, form attractive images. To the photographer their names may not matter, their photogenic properties do.

To many people the most obvious characteristic of a flowering plant is its colour. It is the task of the plant photographer to handle the properties of colour in an appropriate way. For example, is it the purpose of the photograph to show off the colour to best advantage? If so, what kind of light is going to make this possible. What kind of background is going to be appropriate? On the other hand, if the colour is important only because of its setting, then what is the nature of that setting? Does it include colours that will clash or are they complementary to the colour of the main subject? Colour clashes not only detract from the appeal of a photograph, they may also be unfortunate in gardening terms.

TIP– *In order to show off a colour to best advantage, photograph in bright sunlight.*

This advice may be contrary to accepted practice, but if the subject is a strong colour, such as red, orange or bright yellow, there is nothing like direct sunlight to bring out that colour in a vivid and vibrant way. This manner of portrayal can be further increased by using a colour-saturated film, such as Fujichrome Velvia.

Plants come in all shapes and sizes. There are those that are deep from front to back, and those that have very little depth, especially those that grow up a wall or fence. There are tall plants and there are short plants. There are branching plants and there are single-stemmed plants. The variety is endless. What is important is that the photographic technique is matched to a plant's shape, size and structure.

TIP– *If you have a single-lens reflex camera with aperture control, set the aperture at f/16 or f/22 when photographing plants that are deep from front to back.*

The higher the f-number the greater the depth of field. It is necessary to be a bit careful here, for there may be a

This image provides a complete contrast to the previous one. There is only one colour, green. There is no direct sunlight, and yet the shape and texture of the large fern are perfectly recorded, as is its habitat within this woodland area. The photograph was taken in the gardens of the Villa Carlotta, Northern Italy, whilst it was raining. Somehow the rain added the right note to the environmental mood.

The viewpoint has been chosen so as to pick up the radiating habit of this hebe. The camera was placed on a tripod and an aperture of f/16 was used in order to obtain a sufficient depth of field. The shutter speed was a slow 1/8 second but in the absence of any wind this did not matter. The film is Fujichrome Velvia Pro (ISO 50), and three exposures were made. The first was at the meter reading, the second was a little over-exposed and the third a little under-exposed (a technique known as 'bracketing exposures'). It so happens that the first, which was made true to the reading given by the light meter built in to the camera, was also the best at reproducing the natural colours.

trade-off with some lenses between using a high f-number and losing lens quality. Some lenses give their best quality images (i.e. sharpest images) in the aperture range f/8 to f/16. To go beyond f/16 may improve depth of field but, perversely, it may cause a degradation in image quality.

Using these higher f-numbers will usually mean using a slow shutter speed. So slow, in fact, that it is necessary to use a tripod in order to avoid camera shake. However, the use of a slow shutter speed leads to another problem, and this is probably the greatest problem faced by all plant and flower photographers – movement of the plant as a result of wind blowing through the garden.

TIP– If the wind is blowing and moving the plant (or its flowers), don't even think of taking a photograph, you would not be satisfied with the result, unless you can provide some shelter from that wind.

There are several ways of dealing with this problem. The first is to shrug your shoulders and come back when the plant is still. The second is to sacrifice depth of field and go for a faster shutter speed. The third is to erect a wind shield to provide the plant with shelter from the wind while you are taking a photograph. This shield can be a sheet of hardboard, or similar material, which could be covered

with a reflective material in order to allow some reflected light to reach the plant at the same time. The shield could also be in the form of a translucent tent which can be placed over the plant. In this case the camera lens can be pointed at the plant through a hole in the side of the tent. The reason for providing a translucent tent is to allow diffuse light to reach the plant whilst keeping the wind away. In some circumstances this diffuse light may be a better light than direct sunlight for photography (e.g. when harsh shadows need to be eliminated), and thereby two purposes are served: the plant is shielded from the wind and the lighting conditions are improved.

It has to be said that I have never yet seen anyone using a shield or protective tent in a garden belonging to someone else. Whilst plant photographers do carry reflectors, I don't know any that carry translucent tents! So, whilst the idea is a good one, it seems that it is only practised at home.

The second most photogenic property of a plant, after colour, is probably its texture. There is a real difference, for example, between the texture of a leafy plant and a twiggy plant. Texture can also be found in the bark of a tree or even in leaves, providing interesting subjects for photography.

The structure of this rhododendron is that of a branching habit with broad leaves. Spaces normally fall between the branches, although when it is in flower we are more conscious of its glorious blooms than of the precise nature of its structure. The use of a very fast film (Fujichrome Provia 1600 Pro) has allowed the camera to be hand-held without any danger of camera shake – an important factor given the poor light at the time. However, the poor abilities of this film to record detail within a wide range of brightness levels has caused the gaps between the branches to go completely black, and it has thereby emphasised them.

Right: Although we cannot see the whole of this silver birch the photograph tells us a great deal both about the tree itself and its setting (within the grounds of Burford House, Shropshire, England). The trunk does not branch until a point about seven feet (about two metres) above the ground, and then a whole set of branches spray out as if from one point.

Left: In order to see the detail of the texture of the trunk and branches of a tree it is necessary to get in close. It also helps to choose a portion with a low-angle light falling across it. In this case it had been raining and the whole trunk was glistening as though the rain and the overcast sky had combined to bring out the richness of its colour. There is always a limit set by the camera lens as to how close you can get and still keep the subject in focus.

Right: The side-on sunlight has caused the irregularities in the bark to throw shadows that help to pick out its coarse texture.

Photographing texture with success relies very heavily on having good lighting conditions. Normally texture will be photographed in a low-angled light, such as in the early morning or late afternoon. Not only is this a softer light than the light of the middle of the day, but its low angle allows little shadows to develop that pick out minor undulations on the surface of a plant thereby helping to define its texture.

Another characteristic of plants is their shape. They may be bushy, elongated, round, oval, conical or lie flat to the ground. One way of defining this in a photograph is to concentrate on the branching structure of the plant. This can be done by photographing the plant as a whole or it may be done through selecting a typical portion of the plant and photographing only that.

These yellow tulips stand out because they are in the sun whilst the background is in shade.

There are two main methods for making a plant stand out from its background. The first is to photograph the plant when it is in the direct sunlight and the background is in shadow. The second way, and this can be applied when the plant and its background catch an equal amount of light, is to make sure the plant is sharply in focus and the background is not. This technique is known as differential focusing. This is achieved by using an f-number that allows sufficient depth of field for the plant to be adequately in focus from front to back, but renders the background out of focus. It is the opposite of trying to make sure that everything is in sharp focus from the front to the back of the photograph.

TIP– Try focusing on the plant with an aperture of f/5.6 if you want to achieve differential focus between a plant and its background.

If the aperture is set at f/5.6 and the lens is focused on the mid-point of the plant (measured from front to back) and the next background object is more than six feet away (about two metres) then it is likely that the plant will be in focus and the background will not. A differential focus between plant and background will have been achieved.

If the leaves of a plant are large enough it may be possible to fill the whole of an image with nothing but the leaf, or even just a portion of the leaf.
The veins in the leaf show its structure and the closeness of the veins is partly responsible for the coarse texture of the leaf surface.

The decision was made to slightly under-expose this pair of leaves so that the detail of the leaf texture would not be lost. The image relies on the small shadows of the leaf structure to portray the detailed nature of the leaf surface.
The Fujichrome Velvia Pro (ISO 50) is a very fine-grained film, and this also helped to provide a faithful record of the very fine detail.

PHOTOGRAPHING FLOWERS

This rose was isolated from its background by making sure that it was more than six feet (two metres) away from the background, and by using a comparatively low f-number (f/5.6) so that the flower could be kept in focus but the background would lie outside the depth of field. The difference in the colours of the flower and the background also help to make the flower stand out.

The photography of flowers has great appeal and yet it seems so difficult to obtain good results. Let us look at some of the reasons why good results may be elusive.

The first problem to deal with is the wind, which always seems to be blowing so that the result is a blurred image. The way to overcome this is to use a faster shutter speed. By exposing the film for only a fraction (say 1/250) of a second there is a chance that the flower may not have moved far enough to look blurred on the photograph. Even then there may only be a small part of the flower in focus, while the rest is not. The cause of this is the large aperture (low f-number) that has to be used with the fast shutter speed in order to give a correct exposure to the flower. It is in these factors that most of our disappointment will be based.

But there are ways in which we can give ourselves a better chance of success, as the next four tips indicate.

TIP– *Choose a film that reacts fairly quickly to the light (i.e. one with a fairly high ISO value).*

There is a compromise here too, for the faster the film the less capable it is of giving fine levels of detail. However, modern colour films are good enough to allow adequate levels of detail, for most purposes, with films having an ISO

Left: Although these tulips are set within a shady area of Coton Manor Gardens in Northamptonshire, England, it makes a better photograph to wait for the moment when they are illuminated by the sun. Enough of their surroundings are included for their environmental context to be clear, and yet this is still a portrait of the flowers themselves.

Below: Flowers are often best photographed where they are growing. What makes this a flower photograph rather than a plant photograph is the way that the poppies dominate the image through the brilliance of their colour.

The context of this water lily flower is quite clear, as its form and colour. A telephoto lens was necessary to allow the photograph to be taken without disturbing the frog, and this required a tripod in order to prevent camera shake.

of up to 400. Remember, the higher the ISO number the less you will have to lose in depth of field (i.e. the less you will have to descend to low f-numbers) as you use faster shutter speeds. Once you use films faster than ISO 400 there may be a noticeable degradation in the amount of detail that can be precisely recorded.

TIP– *Place the camera on a sturdy tripod.*

The obvious reason for doing this is to reduce the amount of camera shake that we introduce when trying to hold the camera still at slow shutter speeds. As a general rule do not try to hand-hold a camera at shutter speeds slower than 1/125 second. There is another reason why a tripod helps to achieve greater success. When we are focusing on a flower it is the backwards and forwards motion of the camera that is as critical as any sideways wobble that is introduced through camera shake. By placing the camera on a tripod this motion is eliminated and the camera remains focused

A single yellow flower standing in the sun and set against a dark and out-of-focus background is always going to yield a dynamic photograph. It was important to get the correct exposure on the poppy to record the delicate nature of its petals and some of the crinkly detail within them. It helps in cases like this if your camera has a 'spot' meter which enables you to determine the correct exposure for a small part of the picture. In this case an exposure reading was taken from the yellow flower and the rest of the image was left to look after itself. In addition a low f-number (f/5.6) was used in order to throw the background out of focus.

This viola 'Floral Dance' was caught in direct early evening sunlight in order to capture the brilliance of the orange petals.

Isolating the plumes of this astilbe was achieved once again by using an aperture of f/5.6 which meant that the more distant background would be out of focus. The dark background also helps to form a contrast to the brightness of the flowers that helps them to stand out. The camera was turned on to its side so that the long axis of the picture is parallel to the long axis of the flower, which provides the scope for showing more of the flowerhead.

on the point we have selected – even if there is a need to leave the camera and walk over to the plant in order to remove an unwanted item.

TIP– *Concentrate on flower photography early in the morning.*

Not only is the light softer and kinder to most flowers at this time, but if the day is to have a wind-free period it is often in the early mornings before the sun starts to heat the land and cause thermal currents to be set in motion. (Unfortunately this tends only to be true during a period of anticyclonic weather!).

TIP– *Walk up to a flower once every two hours throughout the day and see how it looks when the sun is in different positions in the sky.*

In this picture of a poppy with its fragile and translucent petals, the background has been kept light and airy. It is still out of focus so that the poppy will stand out. This photograph was taken in a wild flower meadow, and there was no attempt to remove the flower or to alter its environment in any way. The choice was made to go for as low an angle as possible so that the sunlight could be seen coming through the petals.

This photograph epitomises the first law of flower photography: 'keep it simple'. By concentrating on the flower and making sure that it had a complementary colour for its background, kept deliberately out of focus, attention becomes concentrated on the flower. The result is an almost three-dimensional effect.

Here the background has been allowed to go black. The sunlight striking the yellow stamens helps them to stand out from the red of the petals. A 'spot' meter reading was taken on the flower, to ensure that it had an acceptable exposure, knowing that the background, which was in shadow, would be completely under-exposed. The result is that the flowerhead stands out well from its background.

It pays to spend some time looking around a flower in order to establish the best angle of view. With this clematis the best angle was from behind looking towards the sky. It shows the translucent nature of the petals and the shapes within the structure of the flower.

There is an enormous difference, for example, between a flower which has the sun shining directly upon it and that same flower when the sun is shining through its petals. This simple exercise in observation will make more difference to the way you view the photography of flowers than any other single thing that you can do.

A fifth contribution to greater success is to make a wind shield and to place it alongside or over the flower in order to cut out the disturbing effect of the wind.

A final approach, if all else fails, is to take the flower indoors and photograph it there. This takes us into the realms of still life and table-top photography. It may also cause problems with those who do not believe that flowers should be picked and taken away. Let me make it quite clear, I would NEVER take a flower (or plant) from the wild. The only place to photograph wild plants is in their natural habitat. The only responsible treatment of habitat is to

Using close-up techniques it becomes possible to isolate details of a flower. The flower in this case was so deep that it was impossible to establish an aperture that would allow the whole of the flower to be in focus. It seemed better to identify a part of the flower that was typical of the flower as a whole, so the stamens and some of the petals were chosen. A plain card was placed behind the flower, so as to remove any background distractions, and some water droplets were sprayed on to the petals in order to increase the photogenic effect.

The pattern of the petals on this rose, together with their colour, provided an appealing subject for close-up photography. The camera was placed on a tripod and a macro lens was used.

The appeal of this poppy lies in the detail of its petals and the structure around its centre. In order to get in as close as this it is necessary to have a macro-lens or some form of close-up attachment that can be placed between the lens and body on your camera. In effect, this means having a single-lens reflex camera rather than a compact camera. With the latter it just is not possible to get in this close and retain the flower in focus.

leave it as you find it. The only things you should take away is your memories and your photographs.

HINT– *The best source of flowers for indoor and table-top photography is probably your local florist.*

The advantages of using your local florist as a source for flowers to photograph include the ability to choose perfect blooms. It is amazing how a blemish in a flower shows up in a photograph. Other benefits include the availability of flowers out of season, so photography can go on throughout the year. The range of colours and colour combinations that the florist can supply may be greater than your own garden, and this increases the range of photographic opportunities available.

Once you start to photograph individual flowers it won't be long before you want to get in really close. There are beautiful images to be obtained by filling the frame with nothing but flower petals. In order to be successful, techniques of close-up photography have to be employed. The reader can do no better than to refer to Joseph Meehan *The Art of Close-up Photography (Fountain Press, 1994)*, for a full account of the techniques and equipment required for making detailed photographs of flowers.

APPROPRIATE CAMERAS

The reason why a discussion of cameras has been left until now is that you need to be clear as to the kind of garden and plant photography that you want to do before you can decide on the equipment that is appropriate for the task.

The discussion so far has taken us from the photography of gardens in general to smaller and smaller portions of the whole, until we are down to close-up photography of flowers and portions of flowers. You have to decide where your interests lie. The real break-point in terms of equipment lies between the desire to photograph gardens, borders and flower beds in their wider expanse, and the desire to get in closer and record some of the finer details. For general photographs a compact camera with a high quality lens may be perfectly adequate, in the case of close-up photography more versatile equipment in the form of a single-lens reflex camera with interchangeable lenses may be required. If the search is for the ultimate in image quality then it starts to be necessary to think of a medium format camera that creates much larger negatives and transparencies.

Left: The barrier of close-focus distance was met in the case of these leaves. I wanted to show the wonderful lime-greens that were so well illuminated by the sun. In order to do this I wanted to fill the image with just one or two leaves. It just was not possible because the camera had a fixed focus 35mm lens (as many compact cameras do) so I had to be content with the closest that the camera would allow. The same restrictions in terms of closeness and image size applies to these hosta leaves (right). It would have been good to have had them big and bold in the photograph, the fixed focal length 35mm lens just would not allow it. Bodnant Gardens in North Wales.

55

COMPACT CAMERAS

There are many keen gardeners who use a compact camera for garden and plant photography. At least so it seems from observing people visiting gardens which are open to the public. They clearly enjoy gardens and want to take photographs either as a record or as a means of making a beautiful photographic image of a beautiful garden scene.

The question which is bound to be asked, however, is whether or not a simple compact camera is adequate for the task. There is no point in spending a lot of money on a more advanced camera system if it is not needed.

A compact camera is usually fully automated, has a single lens, carries a built-in flash gun, has a built-in exposure meter, and takes a 35mm film. An APS camera may share these features except that it does not take a standard 35mm film. On some compacts the lens has a fixed focal length, usually in the range 28-60mm. On others the lens may have a 'zoom' property so that the focal length of the lens can be varied allowing the user to determine whether they want to 'zoom-in' (i.e. use the telephoto end of the

This view within the Bodnant Gardens, North Wales (National Trust) was taken with a compact camera having a lens with a fixed focal length of 35mm. The limitations of a fixed focal length is that the only way to change the composition is to move the camera. it is not possible to zoom-in as you might with a telephoto lens.

Here, in the Tivoli Gardens near Rome, Italy, the use of a compact camera with a telephoto lens has allowed zooming-in to take place. This has made it possible to let the waterfall dominate most of the picture area.

focal lengths) or to 'zoom-out' (i.e. use the wide-angle end of the range of lens focal lengths). Such lenses usually have a focal length range somewhere between 35-110mm.

Whilst it is an undoubted advantage to have a zoom facility on a lens, there is also a drawback in the case of most compact cameras which relates to the smallest aperture that is available to the lens at its maximum telephoto range. As the zoom moves from wide-angle towards telephoto the available maximum aperture (i.e. the f-number) changes from a smaller to a larger number. In other words the aperture becomes smaller. For example, a zoom lens with a range from 38-90mm may have an aperture of f/3.5 at the 38mm (wide-angle) end of the range but only an f/7.5 aperture at the 90mm (telephoto) end of the range. These changes may vary in detail from one camera to another, but the effect is the same: as the aperture gets smaller the shutter speed has to become slower in order to allow enough light to reach the film (for a correct exposure), and the result may well be a speed too slow to prevent camera shake or to 'stop' the movement produced by the wind.

24mm lens

35mm lens

50mm lens

75mm lens

A further limitation of many compact cameras is that they do not allow you any aperture control, and hence you have no control over depth of field. This is one of the main reasons why a compact camera can provide only limited success in plant photography.

THE 35MM SINGLE LENS REFLEX (SLR)

There are many other photographic books which provide a more detailed account of the nature of the 35mm SLR than is possible here. All that can be given is a brief resume of their main characteristics as they affect garden and plant photography.

Some of these features have been mentioned already. The ability to change lenses means that the lens can be matched to the particular situation. For general garden photography a wide-angle lens (say a 28mm or a 35mm focal length lens) will provide a comparatively broad vista. For flower beds and borders the standard (or 'normal') 50mm focal length lens is often the best. For closer work a modest telephoto lens (in the range 70-180mm focal length) can be useful. For photographing plant details a macro lens will provide image detail (up to a 1:1 magnification).

How close you can get to a plant will depend on the characteristics of your lens rather than on the type of camera you are using. Sometimes the standard lens, as here, is sufficient if the subject is large enough. For smaller plants you need the facility to get in closer while still remaining in focus.

Previous pages :
These four photographs illustrate the effect of using lenses having different focal lengths. The broadest view of the garden is obtained with a 24mm wide-angle lens. Some of the curvature which appears in the edge of the lawn is a result of distortion introduced by the small focal length of this lens. As the focal length increases (35mm, 50mm and 75mm) this distortion disappears, the field of view narrows, and the composition becomes tighter.

In order to gain maximum sharpness the camera has been placed on a tripod, the lens was set at a focal length of f/22 and the focusing distance set manually to the hyperfocal distance. Just for once it was also a calm day.

The group of lenses known as 'zoom' lenses provide some of these properties within one lens. At the extreme it is possible to have one lens the focal length of which can be continuously varied from 35mm to 200mm. This gives a wide-angle and a telephoto capability without changing the lens.

There is a further function which is extremely useful in garden and plant photography, and which is found on some SLR cameras, and that is a depth of field preview facility. This is how it works. When you look through the viewfinder of an SLR camera the amount of brightness is determined by the maximum aperture available on the lens, for it is this aperture which is being used by the camera to give you the through-the-lens view of what you

Above: Not all of these snowdrops are in focus because the depth of field is too shallow. This is a common problem in close-up photography.

want to photograph. However, you are interested in what the view will look like at the aperture which you have selected for taking the photograph. In particular you need to know how much of your photograph will be in focus. In other words, what is the depth of field that can be obtained at the selected aperture. The depth of field preview button, when pressed, changes the lens to the aperture at which the photograph will be taken so that you can see, through the viewfinder, what is sharp and what is not. This is an important feature, for you may decide that the depth of field really is not adequate at the chosen aperture and that it is necessary for you to select a higher f-number in order to increase the depth of field.

Left: Sometimes it adds a great deal to a photograph if you can include information about the setting of a garden. This is the garden of the Palazzo Sasso Hotel, Ravello, near Amalfi, Italy. By raising the angle of the camera it has been possible to include the mountainous setting within which this garden occurs.

Most single-lens reflex cameras come with a built-in exposure meter. These meters are usually designed to measure the intensity of light in such a way that dominance is given to the central part of the photograph. That is fine for general photography with an even light across a scene that has little variation in light and dark. Reality is not always like that, and the photographer has to learn to recognise those situations when the exposure meter is likely to give a reading other than the one which may be best for the purposes intended.

Some garden and plant photographers argue vociferously that to get the best results possible it is necessary to use a medium format camera. The benefits are twofold: the size of the original image is larger, and therefore it is possible to obtain a greater enlargement without the degradation that would take place if a 35mm original was used, and secondly, using a medium format camera is a slower process (than using either a compact camera or an SLR 35mm camera) and this forces greater care on the photographer when it comes to image composition.

Both of these points are true. If you are dissatisfied with the quality of your enlargements made from the smaller format, then think not only about moving to a medium format but also in terms of changing your present 35mm outfit for one with greater optical quality in its lenses. You may want to retain the versatility and comparatively less cumbersome state of using the smaller format whilst improving quality. Moving up to a higher quality lens system may be a better answer for you than moving to medium format.

Above: The foxglove in this medium format image has been set against the dark background, while the gnarled trunk of the crab apple tree provides a partial frame.

Right: These pelargoniums were taken with a medium format (6 x 6 cms) camera. This necessitated the use of a tripod which gave much better control over composition than is possible when a camera is hand-held.

Close-ups such as these are only possible with either a special attachment or a macro lens. In these examples a macro lens was used. When working so close to the flower the available depth of field is very shallow, and focusing has to be done extremely carefully.
This is where the manual operation allowed by some SLR cameras is better than the automatic focusing.
It helps if you keep the back of the camera parallel to the face of the flower. Another problem may be that the

The choice over camera is yours, but if you want close-ups and freedom in composition, then (despite the competence of many versatile compact cameras) you will be drawn towards a single-lens reflex system. As to format, the best thing to do is to try out both the 35mm and the medium format and see which best suits your own style.

CLOSE-UPS AND PLANT PORTRAITS

In order to achieve photographs that show plant or flower detail it is necessary to either have a macro lens (which may be able to provide an image on film which is the same size as the object being photographed), or to have an attachment that allows detail to be recorded. The latter may be in the form of a reversing ring (that allows the lens to be used the 'wrong' way round), an extension tube (or bellows) that is placed between the camera body and the lens, or a close-up lens that can be screwed on to the front of the camera lens. All of this is discussed more fully in *The Art of Close-Up Photography* by Joseph Meehan (Fountain Press, 1994).

SOME USEFUL EQUIPMENT

Reference has been made already to the value of using a tripod, a light reflector, and a wind shield. It is unnecessary to dwell on these again here. Instead a short discussion is provided on the only other useful piece of equipment that has so far not received much of a mention, and that is a filter (or rather filters) placed in front of the lens.

For general-purpose garden photography, and indeed for all photography, it is worth keeping a UV (ultra-violet) or a 1B filter permanently mounted in front of the lens.

TIP– *Use the screw-on variety.*

The purpose of this filter is to cut out unwanted ultra-violet light. However, it also serves to protect the front element of the camera lens from scratches and dirt. Since the UV filter does not decrease the intensity of the light passing through it, there is no reduction in the amount of light reaching the film. This is not always the case with filters, so be warned, some filters do decrease the amount of light and therefore require either a larger aperture or a longer exposure time than without them.

Left: The use of a UV filter does not affect the colours recorded on film.

Right: Even though this flower study was made indoors, a UV filter still covered the lens in order to provide constant protection to the lens surface.

Of the whole range of filters that are available the ones that are likely to be the most useful in garden and plant photography are a polarising filter, a soft-focus filter, and possibly a warm-up filter.

A plant portrait using a polarising filter to intensify both the blue of the sky and the yellow of the daffodil.

THE POLARISING FILTER

On a sunny day a polarising filter placed in front of the camera lens will, according to how you use it, increase the depth of blue in the sky and intensify the colour of plants, especially those containing yellow. This filter can also reduce the amount of reflection from leaves and water surfaces (e.g. pond or a lake).

TIP– Obtain a circular polarising filter that fits your camera lens and rotate it as you look through the viewfinder of your SLR. You will notice the change in colour saturation and/or the amount of reflections. Choose a setting that you find suits the way in which you want to take a picture.

A soft-focus (or diffusion) filter was used on these ferns on the floor of the Yosemite Valley in California, USA. The soft strands of the leaves seemed to be crying out for the diffusion treatment.

THE SOFT-FOCUS FILTER

A soft-focus (or diffusion) filter is designed to give a somewhat 'dreamy' effect to the picture. It is an effect which suits some plant portraits.

TIP– When doing plant portraits take one exposure without a soft-focus filter and one with, you can decide on which you prefer when you see the results.

HINT– The best effects are obtained when a soft-focus filter is used on a flower whose colour is in pastel shades.

TIP– It is also possible to obtain a soft-focus effect by other means. One is to breathe on the front of the lens (though more likely this will be on the UV filter that is in place to protect the lens) and take the picture before the lens clears again.

TIP– Another approach is to smooth-out a small amount of petroleum jelly ('vaseline') on the front of the UV filter and to see what the effects are on the final image.

HINT– In time you will be able to smear the vaseline in such a way as to get the results that you actually want.

Here a centre-spot/soft-focus filter shows the spring growth on an apple tree. The new growth was placed in the clear area of the filter and the rest of the tree was given the soft-focus treatment by the rest of the filter.

THE WARM-UP FILTER

Warm-up filters give a slight orange cast to a photograph. This gives the impression that a sunny 'glow' is present. Warm-up filters come in a range of strengths, but at its most intense the orange glow becomes a colour cast that is entirely unnatural. The most useful warm-up filters are designated 81a, 81b, and 81c (with the 81c providing a stronger warm-up effect than 81a).

A COLOUR-SPOT FILTER

Finally mention may be made of the spot-filter (or colour-spot filter as it is sometimes called). This consists of a central portion that has no optical effect on light, but around this centre the effect is that of a soft-focus or diffusion filter. You need to try this out at various apertures to see the range of effects that can be achieved, you may or may not like what you get.

Above: Somehow this picture of a portion of a bluebell wood doesn't work for me. The boundary between the clear centre and the diffused edge is too noticeable. This is not so at all apertures, so remember to experiment until you get the effect that you want.

Right: This portrait of a red tulip set apart from the rest of its group has again been given the centre-spot/soft-focus margins treatment. The effect is 'different', it is a matter of taste whether or not it is also found to be pleasing.

FILM CHOICE

The number of garden and plant photographers that use black and white film is limited, for the obvious reason that so much of the information about a plant is contained in its colour. Somehow gardens, plants, flowers and colour go together, even if the only colour is green and all of the variation lies in tones and textures.

Most users of compact cameras, requiring prints that can be handled, shown round and mounted in an album, will use colour negative film. The same will be true of SLR users, unless they want to view their images as slides through a projector in which case colour transparency film is the obvious choice.

Colour negative film has a greater exposure latitude than colour transparency film. It is therefore more tolerant of slight errors in exposure. It is a good medium if you want colour prints and are not concerned about projection.

Colour transparency film, however, is the choice to make if you want to see your work published. Most magazine and book publishers prefer transparencies preferably on fine-grained and colour-saturated films.

Left: Fujichrome Velvia (ISO 50) is known for its colour saturation properties, especially the greens and the reds. If this is too powerful for your tastes try another manufacturer (e.g. Kodachrome 64), or try a colour negative film, many of which are more muted in their rendition of colour.

Right: Fujichrome Velvia (ISO 50) is used here both for its 'punch' in terms of showing red against a green background, but also because of its fine-grain characteristics that allow considerable enlargement without image degradation.

This brings us then to the main components of a colour film. These are its speed, the ability to cope with a range of light intensities (i.e. latitude), its colour saturation and its sharpness, with the latter somewhat dependent on the grain-size characteristics of the emulsion used on the film, which in turn is closely related to film speed. In general the faster the film (i.e. the higher its ISO value) the coarser the grain size and the less sharp the final image. Also, a faster film has less ability to cope with variations in light intensity (i.e. the latitude of the film decreases with film speed).

Colour saturation varies more with manufacturer than it does with any of the other film characteristics. For example, Fujichrome Velvia is known for its strong representation of colours (especially the greens and the reds) and is said to be a highly colour-saturated film.

It could be argued that for garden and plant photography, where the amount of available light may sometimes be very limited, it is best to use as fast a film as possible. In this way long exposure times (and the camera shake that goes with it) can be avoided. Up to a point this is true. With colour negative film it is quite possible to obtain perfectly acceptable results in terms of image sharpness, with film rated at ISO400. With colour transparency film the same is true up to speeds of ISO200.

Kodak Ektachrome (100SW) is a transparency film designed to have slightly 'warm' characteristics. It certainly makes the greens more muted than would have been the case if Fujichrome Velvia had been used to photograph these hostas.

Colour saturation is a characteristic of several of the films in the Fujichrome range. Here Fujichrome Astia richly records the colours of the rhododendrons and azaleas at Bodnant Gardens, North Wales (National Trust).

Fujichrome Provia (ISO 100) is twice as fast as Velvia, retains some of the colour saturation of Velvia, and is capable of considerable enlargement before sharpness degrades.

Fujichrome Astia (ISO 100) is a more recent introduction from Fuji than either Velvia or Provia. It has very fine grain and is probably a little more muted in terms of colour saturation.

Kodak Ektachrome Pro (ISO 200) has a useful speed for use when the wind is blowing and a moderately fast shutter speed is required. The saturation of the colours (here the greens) is far less than on the slower Fuji films.

Fujichrome Provia (ISO 400)
is twice as fast as the ISO
200 films, giving a further
advantage of shutter speed
under poor light or windy
conditions.
The colour saturation is good
but there is a greater fall
away in definition with size
of enlargement.

Fujichrome Provia (ISO 1600)
is a very special film. It has
a very fast rating, can cope
with very poor light, has a
coarse grain structure, but is
very bad at coping with more
than a modest amount of
variation in light intensities.

That is why it quickly throws
the shadow areas on this
tree trunk into complete
blackness.
However, in doing so it
increases the sense of bark
roughness and the gnarled
state of the tree.

At higher speeds, and ISO1600 is at the extreme end of the range, grain is noticeable (if not irritating), colour saturation is weak, latitude is very limited, and when the sun shines brightly the settings of aperture and shutter speed required for a correct exposure may fall outside the range available on the camera! On the other hand under very poor lighting conditions Fujichrome Provia ISO1600 can save the day. There are also some subjects, such as the bark of rough trees, or an outcrop of sandstone in a rock garden, when the additional grain in the film can give a pleasing image.

The choice is very much yours. Be prepared to experiment with different films, then choose the one that suits you and the situation in which you are doing your photography.

Above: The tulips in the foreground are brightly lit by the afternoon sun. The film on this occasion is Fujichrome Provia 1600, which is a very fast film. It is also a comparatively grainy film, and one with a small tolerance of variations in light and shade. You will notice how black the shadow areas have gone. This would not have been the case with a slower film. A slower film would have retained some of the detail in these areas.

Right: The tendency for Fujichrome films to record greens rather vividly can be used to advantage when green is the colour of the main object (in this case a fern) in the photograph.

WHOSE GARDEN?

Right: In the formal areas of Butchart Gardens, Vancouver Island, Canada, it is difficult to minimise the people because they are bound to feature larger in the more confined space. In a sense these visitors are so much a part of the place that they do not seem entirely out of place.

Left: Gardens which are open to the public, such as the Butchart Gardens, Vancouver Island, Canada, provide a rich opportunity for garden and plant photography. Be careful not to abuse this privilege, other photographers also want to be allowed to enjoy the gardens. The dilemma which we all face in such gardens is whether or not to include the people that abound in such places. Here the people occupy minimal space and command minimal attention.
They do, however, provide a sense of scale within these magnificent gardens.

Every encouragement has been given to use your own garden as much as possible for garden and plant photography. You have only to visit a garden which is open to the public to realise how many people also enjoy taking photographs in gardens other than their own. So, here are a few hints and tips on photographing such gardens.

There are three main difficulties to contend with in public gardens, these are: other people, restricted access and the nature of the light whilst you are there.

TIP– *If you want to keep people out of your pictures concentrate on the flower beds and their content rather than broad vistas of whole gardens.*

If it is necessary to include areas through which the public pass, then patience is the only answer. Eventually a moment usually comes when everyone is hidden behind trees or bushes and the view is clear, but don't wait too long for such moments may be fleeting.

TIP– *Set the camera up on a tripod and make sure of the exposure settings and composition whilst people are around, and then the only thing that remains is to fire the shutter when people have left the scene.*

Because of restricted access and the general limitation on viewpoints within gardens (e.g. you ought to stay off the flower beds!), good compositions have to come from the care with which you place plants relative to each other within the image frame.

HINT– Concentrate on using plants to give a strong foreground and keep unwanted patches of bare sky, branches and other clutter out of the picture.

Most of us visit public gardens for a day, where the day is chosen for reasons other than the kind of light that will exist when we go. We have to "take it as it comes". This inevitably means that we are there in the middle of the day when the light is at its most intense and least likely to generate a photogenic situation. There are some photographs which are best taken at this time of day, including portraits of flowers with intense colours. However, in general the low-angle, softer and subdued light which occurs at either end of the day provides more advantageous photographic conditions. In addition, morning mists, dew and condensation droplets on plants (especially in autumn and winter) soon disappear as the sun rises.

Many public gardens include structural elements that are an aid in photographic composition.
This archway at Sudeley Castle in Gloucestershire, England provides a setting for the flowers in the foreground and provides a frame for the garden beyond. The problem was that people kept walking through the arch. The only answer was to set everything up whilst people were around and to take the photograph the moment the arch was clear of people.

Water forms a very important element in many public gardens. Use them for reflections and to portray calmness (as here at Bodnant Gardens in North Wales).

In many public gardens ponds have a formal setting, and it is necessary to include some of this setting in order to give the water a proper context. Sudeley Castle, Gloucestershire, England.

When a large number of people are around concentrate on a portion of a pond to which people have no access. Hidcote Manor Gardens (National Trust), Gloucestershire, England.

The flowers on these three plants require a soft light to bring out the best in their colours and to diminish the problems of heavy shadows. They were all taken either early in the day, with a soft low light (as in the case of the pink poppies), in the shade (the lilies), or with a small amount of bounced light whilst the main plant stood in the shade (the azalea).

Above: Occasionally the water is a part of a strongly architectural form to the garden, as in the Japanese Garden within the Devonian Gardens, near Edmonton, Canada.

Antirrhinium in soft early morning light.

Gardens of Burford House, Shropshire, in early morning light. The early frost of winter still lingers on the plants, but is soon removed by the mid-morning sun.

TIP– *Try to include at least one end of the day in your visit to public gardens as this will allow you to take advantage of the better photographic light that this provides.*

If, on the other hand, the garden is yours then you can approach its photography in a different way. There is no restriction on the time when you can use good light. There is no restriction on the time of year when you can be there. In fact, you can even change the garden to suit your photography! You find yourself choosing plants for their colour, form and texture, not just for the sake of the garden but also so that you can make an even greater success of your garden and plant photography.

Right: Green is a dominant constituent of many gardens. Look for interesting shapes and isolate them. These ferns were taken in the shade, and because of the poor light a tripod had to be used.

Left: A long view in the Buchart Gardens, Victoria Island, British Columbia. Note how the statue draws the eye into the garden and in so doing provides and extra sense of depth to the view.

Above: There may well be a photograph at the base of a plant, so be prepared to look at all levels. Theses hosta stems growing out of gravel are given an extra sense of

mystery by the misty image. This was achieved by breathing on the lens and taking the exposure before the lens cleared again.

SOME OF THE GARDENS FEATURED IN THIS BOOK

Left: Amongst the formal gardens that delight and provide plentiful photographic opportunities the Tivoli Gardens near Rome has to be a favourite.
These gardens are especially famous for its many water features.

Right: Dell Garden, Bressingham, Norfolk.
The home of Alan Bloom who created this herbaceous garden out of rough land and, in the process, created a wonderful place for garden photographers.

Left: Flower bed in the public gardens along the shore of Lake Geneva, Evian, France. Taken with a compact camera using a telephoto setting and keeping the arms well supported on a post.

Right: Coton Manor Gardens in Northamptonshire include a woodland walk in the bluebell season. Throughout the rest of the year the gardens near to the house are a perpetual delight.

Many of the flower photographs in this book were taken in my own garden. Remember, your own garden is a good place in which to practice your technique and aquire new skills.

Right: Finally, remember that simplicity in composition is the key to success in garden photography. (Coton Manor Gardens, Northamptonshire, England).

Overleaf: The National Trust has many gardens, but of all of them Bodnant Gardens in North Wales are very special, especially the spring display of rhododendrons and azaleas offer much joy to the garden lover and the garden photographer.

INDEX